30-Day Couples Retreat

A Comprehensive Guide to Reconnecting through Holistic Therapy

Katherina & Robert Belmont

CONTENTS

Introduction: The Power of a 30-Day Retreat

Relationships, like gardens, require consistent care, attention, and love. **But what happens when we get busy with life, and our attention diverts elsewhere?** Plants wither, the ground dries up, and what was once a vibrant garden becomes an almost unrecognizable patch of land.

Every couple goes through their own set of challenges, and at times, it feels like the connection is dwindling. This is where a dedicated time for reconnection becomes imperative. Enter: The 30-Day Couples Retreat.

Why 30 days? The science of habit formation and deep connection

It's been scientifically observed that it takes approximately 21 days to form a new habit. While some habits might take longer and others shorter, this general time frame is significant. *"You do not rise to the level of your goals. You fall to the level of your systems."* This quote by James Clear, the author of "Atomic Habits", emphasizes the importance of creating systems or routines. By dedicating 30 days, you not only form a habit but also solidify it. This retreat isn't just about patching things up; it's about creating lasting, positive changes in your relationship.

Additionally, deep connections require time. Time to understand, to communicate, and to truly listen. This retreat provides you with a designated space to make those connections without the rush of everyday life.

The importance of dedicating time for relationship healing

In our fast-paced world, filled with notifications, meetings, and to-do lists, dedicating time solely for one's relationship might seem like a luxury. But in truth, it's a necessity. Relationships are the backbone of our emotional well-being. As Dr. John Gottman, a pioneer in relationship research, once said, *"Every positive thing you do in your relationship is foreplay."* Every moment dedicated to your partner, every effort made towards understanding them, every gesture of love is a step towards a stronger bond.

With this retreat, we aim to provide a comprehensive guide to dive deep into your relationship, explore areas that need attention, and emerge with a stronger, more resilient bond. As you embark on this journey, remember that it's about progress, not perfection. There will be days of revelations and days of challenges, but each day will bring its own reward.

Day 1: Setting Intentions and Ground Rules

Embarking on a journey without a clear map or direction can often lead to feeling lost or overwhelmed. This is why setting clear intentions and ground rules at the beginning of your retreat is pivotal.

Why intentions matter in a retreat

Intention is the driving force behind every action. It's the "why" behind our "what." When we understand our motivations and desires clearly, the path to achieving them becomes more apparent.

In a relationship, both partners come with their own set of intentions and expectations. By setting joint intentions, you create a unified vision, ensuring that you're both walking hand in hand towards a shared destination. It's akin to creating a compass for your retreat. Whenever you feel lost or unsure, you can always revisit your intentions to guide you back on track.

Crafting meaningful intentions for the journey ahead

Setting intentions is not just about listing what you want to achieve. It's a deeper exercise of introspection.

- **Reflect individually:** Before discussing with your partner, take a moment to jot down what you wish to achieve from this retreat. It could be understanding your partner better, learning to communicate effectively, or finding joy in each other's company again.

- **Come together and share:** Once both of you have your individual lists, come together. Share your intentions with each other, and listen actively.

- **Create joint intentions:** After understanding each other's goals, create a list of joint intentions. These are shared goals that both of you agree upon and want to work towards.

Remember, intentions aren't set in stone. They can evolve as you progress in your retreat. What's important is the spirit of alignment and understanding.

Setting boundaries and guidelines for effective communication

While intentions act as the compass, ground rules are the safety gear for your journey. They ensure that discussions remain constructive and that both partners feel respected and heard.

- **Respect is paramount:** Even when disagreements arise, always approach each other with respect. Avoid name-calling or hurtful comments.

- **Active listening:** When one partner speaks, the other listens. It's not about waiting for your turn to speak but genuinely understanding what the other person is saying.

- **Safe word:** If a discussion gets too heated, have a safe word. Whenever one of you uses it, take a break. This ensures that discussions don't escalate into arguments.

- **Stay committed:** Commit to the entire process. Even on days when it feels challenging, remember your intentions and the reason behind this retreat.

The first day is about laying a strong foundation for the days to come. By setting clear intentions and guidelines, you are ensuring that the journey ahead is meaningful and constructive. As renowned relationship expert Esther Perel often says, *"The quality of our relationships determines the quality of our lives."* With Day 1, you're taking a step towards enhancing the quality of your most precious relationship.

Day 2: Active Listening Exercises

"When people talk, listen completely. Most people never listen." - Ernest Hemingway

The human longing to be truly heard is as old as time itself. Imagine the profound connection that takes place when two people genuinely hear each other. When was the last time you felt completely heard? When was the last time you gave your partner that same gift?

The art of truly hearing your partner:

Active listening goes beyond merely hearing words. It's about being present and absorbing the emotions, intentions, and nuances behind what's being said.

- **The Essence of True Listening:** It's not about waiting for your turn to speak. Instead, it's about creating an empathetic connection where you genuinely want to understand what your partner is saying and feeling.

- **Beyond Words:** Understand that communication is not solely verbal. Pay attention to body language, facial expressions, and tone of voice. These non-verbal cues can communicate as much, if not more, than words themselves.

- **The Power of Presence:** Avoid distractions. Put away phones, turn off the TV, and focus solely on your partner. A distracted mind can't actively listen.

Practical exercises for enhancing listening skills:
- **Mirror Exercise:**

  - *How it works:* One partner shares a feeling or an experience. Once they finish, the other partner mirrors or repeats back what they heard without adding any interpretation.

  - *Purpose:* This practice helps ensure that the listener fully grasps what's being shared and offers the speaker a chance to correct any misinterpretations.

- **Non-verbal Communication Focus:**

- *How it works:* Partners sit facing each other in silence, communicating only through facial expressions and body language.

- *Purpose:* This deepens the understanding of non-verbal cues, reminding couples that words are just a fraction of communication.

- **Interruption-free Zone:**

  - *How it works:* Dedicate a time (e.g., 20 minutes) where one person speaks, and the other solely listens. No interruptions allowed.

  - *Purpose:* This helps cultivate patience, teaching both the speaker to articulate thoughts fully and the listener to hold space.

Today's takeaway: Commit to actively listening. By doing so, you're not just hearing words; you're hearing the heart.

Day 3: Exploring Individual Values

"Find people who share your values, and you'll conquer the world together." - John Ratzenberger

Every individual carries a set of values – intrinsic beliefs that dictate behavior, guide decisions, and form our understanding of happiness and purpose. For couples, recognizing, aligning, and celebrating these values can be the foundation of a deep, lasting connection.

Deep dive into personal values:

- **What Are Values?** They are the core principles and standards that matter most to us. Examples include family, honesty, freedom, love, security, adventure, and more.

- **Why They Matter:** Our values influence every aspect of our lives – from daily routines to life-changing decisions. They're the silent drivers behind why we do what we do.

Aligning and understanding differences and similarities:

Understanding your values and your partner's can pave the way for deeper empathy and better conflict resolution.

- **List and Share:**

  - *How it works:* Separately, list down your top 5 values. Share with each other and discuss why they're essential to you.

  - *Purpose:* Helps in understanding core motivations and life drivers.

- **Value Stories:**

  - *How it works:* Share stories from your past (childhood, adolescence, adulthood) that highlight why a particular value means so much to you.

  - *Purpose:* By sharing stories, you're not just explaining a value, but you're giving it context, making it relatable and understandable.

- **Aligning Shared Values:**

  - *How it works:* Identify values that both you and your partner hold dear. Discuss how these shared values can be the pillars of your relationship.

  - *Purpose:* Reinforces the idea that while you're two individuals, there's common ground that can serve as a strong foundation for your journey together.

- **Navigating Differing Values:**

  - *How it works:* Openly discuss values that might not align. Understand that it's okay to have differences. The key is finding ways to respect and acknowledge them without letting them become sources of conflict.

  - *Purpose:* Teaches couples that differences aren't necessarily bad and can be an opportunity for growth and deeper understanding.

Today's takeaway: Your values are the compass that guides your life. Sharing and aligning them with your partner can lead to a journey that's both fulfilling and harmonious.

Day 4: Gratitude Journaling

"Gratitude can transform common days into thanksgivings, turn routine jobs into joy, and change ordinary opportunities into blessings." - William Arthur Ward

In our fast-paced world, it's easy to take our partner's actions and presence for granted. To fortify a bond and truly appreciate the journey together, it's essential to cultivate gratitude actively. And there's no better way to do this than through journaling.

The transformative power of gratitude:

- **The Science Behind It:** Studies have consistently shown that practicing gratitude improves well-being, reduces the risk of depression, heightens relationship satisfaction, and even boosts the immune system.

- **Deepening Connections:** Recognizing and acknowledging the good in your partner can solidify the bond. It's a reminder of why you're on this journey together.

- **Attracting Positivity:** The more gratitude you show, the more you focus on the positive. And as the law of attraction suggests, like attracts like.

Guided prompts to cultivate thankfulness in relationships:

- **Daily Joys:**

  - *Prompt:* Write about a small, everyday moment you shared with your partner that brought you joy.

  - *Purpose:* Helps couples appreciate the mundane and understand that magic can be found in simplicity.

- **Overcoming Challenges:**

  - *Prompt:* Reflect on a challenge both of you faced together and overcame. How did this strengthen your relationship?

  - *Purpose:* To view obstacles not as hindrances but as stepping stones to a deeper connection.

- **Qualities Admired:**

  - *Prompt:* List five qualities in your partner that you deeply admire and are grateful for.

  - *Purpose:* To focus on the positives and acknowledge the value the other brings into the relationship.

- **Memorable Experiences:**

  - *Prompt:* Describe a memory with your partner that always brings a smile to your face.

  - *Purpose:* Reliving joyous moments can rekindle warmth and affection.

- **Dreams and Hopes:**

  - *Prompt:* Share a dream or hope you're grateful to have, knowing your partner is by your side to achieve it.

  - *Purpose:* Affirms that you're a team, ready to take on the world together.

Today's takeaway: Remember, what's taken for granted can eventually be taken away. Regular gratitude journaling can act as an anchor, grounding your relationship in love, respect, and appreciation.

Day 5: Embodied Movement: Dance Therapy

"Dance is the hidden language of the soul." - Martha Graham

While conversations, both verbal and non-verbal, are crucial, sometimes, our bodies need to do the talking. Dance therapy offers couples a chance to break free from verbal constraints, letting emotions flow and connecting on an energetically intimate level.

Letting go through dance:

- **Therapeutic Benefits:** Dance therapy can help improve self-esteem, body image, communication skills, and decrease feelings of isolation. It creates a non-judgmental space to express and understand.

- **Embracing Vulnerability:** Dancing, especially with someone you love, can be an act of vulnerability. Letting go of inhibitions can pave the way for deeper emotional intimacy.

Expressing emotions and rediscovering fun:

- **Mirror Movement:**

  - *How it works:* One partner leads with a dance movement, while the other mirrors it. Swap roles after a few minutes.

  - *Purpose:* Develops a deeper understanding and synchronicity between partners.

- **Emotion Emulation:**

  - *How it works:* One partner calls out an emotion (e.g., joy, sadness, anger), and both dance embodying that feeling.

  - *Purpose:* Allows couples to express feelings they might find hard to verbalize.

- **Freestyle Connection:**

- *How it works:* Play your favorite tunes and dance freely without any rules or steps.

- *Purpose:* Helps in letting go of daily stresses and reconnecting with the joy of each other's company.

- **Recall and Dance:**

  - *How it works:* Think of a fond memory, share it with your partner, and then dance, channeling the emotions of that moment.

  - *Purpose:* Reliving happy moments and integrating them into the present.

- **Silent Dance:**

  - *How it works:* Without music, let your bodies move to their inner rhythm.

  - *Purpose:* Teaches couples to lead and follow intuitively, relying on non-verbal cues.

Today's takeaway: Dance, in its essence, captures the human spirit. It gives freedom to emotions that words might confine. Through dance therapy, couples can discover layers of their relationship previously unexplored, bringing vibrancy and vitality to their connection.

DAY 6: GUIDED VISUALIZATION FOR RELATIONSHIP GOALS

"The best way to predict the future is to create it." - Abraham Lincoln

Visualization has long been used by athletes, entrepreneurs, and artists to enhance performance and achieve desired outcomes. But it's not exclusive to them! Couples can use visualization to manifest their relationship aspirations and strengthen their bond.

Imagining a Shared Future:

- **Science Behind Visualization:** Our brain struggles to differentiate between real and imagined scenarios.

So when you visualize a loving, harmonious relationship, your brain starts laying the foundation for that reality.

- **Manifesting Desires:** By imagining a shared future, you're planting seeds in the universe. Combined with action, these dreams can manifest.

Strengthening Bonds Through Collective Dreams:

- **Shared Spaces:**

  - *Exercise:* Sit with your partner and describe your ideal home. Every room, every detail.

  - *Purpose:* Create a sense of belonging, identifying shared aesthetic tastes and functional preferences.

- **Future Adventures:**

  - *Exercise:* Discuss places you'd love to visit together, imagining every sensation, sight, and sound.

  - *Purpose:* Cultivate a spirit of adventure and togetherness.

- **Celebrating Milestones:**

  - *Exercise:* Visualize future anniversaries or significant dates, detailing the celebration, surroundings, and emotions.

- *Purpose:* Deepen the appreciation of the journey and the milestones achieved together.

- **Life's Achievements:**

  - *Exercise:* Share individual and shared goals, visualizing the moment they're realized.

  - *Purpose:* Reinforces support for each other's aspirations and shared dreams.

Guided Visualization Practice:

- **Setting:** Choose a quiet space, sit back-to-back, and hold hands if comfortable.

- **Breathing:** Start with deep breaths, synchronizing with each other.

- **Guidance:** One partner describes a future scenario, speaking softly. The other listens and imagines. Swap roles after 10 minutes.

- **Sharing:** Discuss the emotions felt during the exercise.

Today's takeaway: The future, while uncertain, offers couples a blank canvas. Through visualization, paint a masterpiece of love, dreams, and shared adventures.

DAY 7: EXPLORING PAST RESOLUTIONS AND HEALING

"The wounds of the past can't be healed with intentions of a future alone; they need to be addressed directly, felt, understood, and processed." - Anonymous

Looking ahead is vital, but understanding and healing from the past is just as crucial. By addressing past hurdles, couples can free themselves from lingering pain, creating a solid foundation for future growth.

Reflecting on Past Hurdles:

- **Benefit of Hindsight:** With time, couples can look back at obstacles more objectively, understanding how they've shaped the relationship's evolution.

- **Shared Growth:** Each hurdle crossed has strengthened the bond. Reflecting on them serves as a reminder of the resilience and growth shared.

Techniques to Heal and Move Forward:

- **Open Dialogue:**

  - *How It Works:* Allocate time for an open conversation about past challenges. Discuss feelings, reactions, and lessons learned.

  - *Purpose:* By speaking openly, couples can ensure no lingering doubts or resentments remain.

- **Emotion Mapping:**

  - *How It Works:* Write down significant challenges faced. For each, detail the emotions felt, both negative and positive.

  - *Purpose:* Visualize the emotional journey, understanding triggers and growth points.

- **Gratitude Practice:**

  - *How It Works:* For each challenge faced, list things you're grateful for that wouldn't have been possible without that experience.

- *Purpose:* Transform negative memories into positive growth experiences.

- **Forgiveness Exercise:**

  - *How It Works:* If mistakes were made, practice verbalizing forgiveness, understanding that everyone is evolving.

  - *Purpose:* Release emotional burdens, allowing for a fresher start.

- **Ritual Release:**

  - *How It Works:* Write down past resentments or hurts on paper. Together, safely burn or bury these papers as a symbolic release.

  - *Purpose:* Rituals can provide a tangible sense of closure, emphasizing the intention to move past old wounds.

Today's takeaway: Relationships, like life, are full of ups and downs. By addressing, understanding, and healing from past challenges, couples pave the way for a healthier, more harmonious future.

Day 8: Mindful Nature Walk

> *"In every walk with nature, one receives far more than he seeks."* - John Muir

Nature has a unique way of grounding us, reminding us of the beauty that exists beyond our daily stresses. As couples, taking a walk in nature offers an opportunity not just for physical activity, but for mental and emotional rejuvenation.

Embracing the Therapeutic Powers of Nature:

- **Natural Calm:** Nature inherently brings peace. The chirping of birds, the rustle of leaves, the gentle flow of water; all work in harmony to create a calming ambiance.

- **Presence and Awareness:** Away from distractions, nature compels you to be present. This act of being wholly in the moment can foster deeper connections between partners.

- **Healing and Renewal:** Nature symbolizes growth, renewal, and cycles of life – powerful metaphors for relationships.

Deepening the Bond Through Shared Experiences:

- **Sensory Exploration:**

  - *Exercise:* While walking, take turns in naming things you can hear, see, smell, feel, and taste. Engage all your senses.

  - *Purpose:* Increases mindfulness and joint appreciation of surroundings.

- **Nature's Metaphors:**

  - *Exercise:* Identify natural elements that resonate with your relationship's journey: a resilient tree, a flowing river symbolizing adaptability, etc.

  - *Purpose:* Recognize and celebrate the growth and nature of your relationship.

- **Silent Segments:**

  - *Exercise:* Dedicate portions of your walk to silence, focusing solely on the environment and your partner's presence.

  - *Purpose:* Encourage non-verbal communication and deep reflection.

- **Nature's Lessons:**

  - *Exercise:* Discuss lessons nature teaches – patience, resilience, growth, and how they can be applied to your relationship.

  - *Purpose:* Draw parallels between nature and relationship dynamics, learning and growing together.

Planning a Mindful Nature Walk:

- **Pick a Scenic Route:** Choose a location that's calming and resonates with both of you – a beach, forest, or park.

- **Disconnect:** Leave phones and gadgets behind or put them on silent. This time is about the two of you and nature.

- **Wear Comfortable Attire:** Ensure you're dressed

appropriately for the weather and location.

- **Take a Moment:** Before starting, stand still, take a few deep breaths, setting the intention to be present.

Today's takeaway: Nature offers a beautiful backdrop to reflect, connect, and grow as a couple. It provides lessons, metaphors, and experiences that can deepen a relationship's bond.

Day 9: Chakra Balancing for Couples

"The thing about chakras is that they are not only energetic but metaphoric. They give language to universal themes everyone must confront." - Anodea Judith

Chakras, the energy centers within our body, play a vital role in our physical, emotional, and spiritual well-being. When aligned and balanced, they allow for the free flow of energy. Couples can embark on a journey of chakra balancing to enhance their connection.

Understanding the Seven Chakras:

- **Root Chakra (Muladhara):** Represents our foundation and feeling of being grounded.

- **Sacral Chakra (Swadhisthana):** Relates to our ability to connect and accept others and new experiences.

- **Solar Plexus Chakra (Manipura):** Symbolizes our ability to be confident and in control.

- **Heart Chakra (Anahata):** Reflects our ability to love.

- **Throat Chakra (Vishuddha):** Centers on our ability to communicate.

- **Third Eye Chakra (Ajna):** Relates to our ability to see the bigger picture.

- **Crown Chakra (Sahasrara):** Represents our ability to connect spiritually.

Exercises to Harmonize Energy Flow:

- **Chakra Meditation:**

  - *How It Works:* Sit back to back in a quiet space, meditating on each chakra's location and color. Visualize energy flowing and chakras aligning.

  - *Purpose:* Cultivates shared energy and understanding between partners.

- **Affirmation Exchange:**

    - *How It Works:* For each chakra, exchange affirmations. For example, for the heart chakra, you might affirm: "I am open to giving and receiving love."

    - *Purpose:* Reinforces positive energy and shared intentions.

- **Yoga Poses:**

    - *How It Works:* Practice couples yoga poses targeting each chakra.

    - *Purpose:* Physically stimulates and balances energy centers.

- **Crystal Healing:**

    - *How It Works:* Place chakra-specific crystals on each energy point while lying down, meditating on each chakra.

    - *Purpose:* Crystals are believed to help in balancing specific chakras.

- **Chakra-based Discussions:**

    - *How It Works:* For each chakra, discuss themes related to it. Discuss grounding for the root chakra, communication for the throat chakra, etc.

- ○ *Purpose:* Encourages deep discussions and understanding related to each chakra's theme.

Today's takeaway: Chakra balancing is more than an energetic exercise; it's a journey of understanding oneself and one's partner on deeper, interconnected levels. Through chakra balancing, couples can find harmony, balance, and a stronger connection.

Day 10: Nutritional Cooking for Emotional Balance

There's a saying that goes, *"The way to a man's heart is through his stomach."* However, for couples looking to reconnect, the route can just as aptly be said to be *"The way to a couple's heart is through shared meals."*

The Connection Between Food and Emotion

Before diving into recipes and cooking, it's pivotal to understand the profound link between what we eat and how we feel. As Virginia Woolf aptly said, "One cannot think well, love well, sleep well, if one has not dined well."

- **Neurotransmitters**: Some foods boost the production of neurotransmitters like serotonin, often called the "feel good" hormone. Eating these foods can elevate our mood and enhance feelings of happiness and contentment.

- **Comfort Foods**: We all have those dishes that remind us of home or happier times. They invoke nostalgia and comfort, often helping us cope during tough times.

- **Shared Meals**: When couples cook together, they are not just preparing food. They're creating memories, fostering understanding, and building a shared experience. This act alone can be a therapeutic and bonding experience.

Foods that Foster Connection

Certain foods have been known to trigger positive emotions or provide an environment conducive to deep conversations. Here's a list:

- **Chocolate**: Contains phenylethylamine, a compound that stimulates the same feeling as falling in love.

- **Berries**: Full of antioxidants, they are great for brain health and overall mood enhancement.

- **Oily Fish**: Rich in omega-3 fatty acids which can help alleviate symptoms of depression and boost mood.

- **Whole Grains**: Steady energy release, keeping mood swings in check.

- **Green Tea**: Contains L-theanine, which can help with relaxation.

Preparing and Sharing a Meal Together

Embarking on this culinary journey as a couple, consider these steps:

- **Plan Together**: This isn't just about one person taking the lead. Discuss what you'd like to make, ensuring it's a meal both will enjoy.

- **Shop Together**: Turn grocery shopping into a date. Enjoy the experience of selecting ingredients together.

- **Cook Together**: Divide tasks. If one is good at chopping while the other excels at sautéing, play to those strengths.

- **Eat Mindfully**: When you finally sit down to eat, do so without distractions. Savor every bite and enjoy the flavors.

- **Reflect on the Experience**: Talk about what you enjoyed most about the cooking process. Share what you felt during each stage.

Today's takeaway: cooking isn't just about eating but about the experience as a whole. It's about teamwork, understanding each other's preferences, and working in harmony.

Day 11: Tantric Breathing Practices

*B*reath. *It's the essence of life.* While it's an involuntary act that sustains us, when used mindfully, it can also enhance intimacy, understanding, and connection between couples. The ancient art of Tantra can be a guiding light for couples seeking deeper intimacy, and at its core lies the practice of breathing.

Deepening Intimacy Through Breath

At a glance, it might seem odd to connect breathing with intimacy, but consider this quote by Thich Nhat Hanh: "The most precious gift we can offer others is our presence. When mindfulness embraces those we love, they will bloom like flowers." Breath is an anchor to the present moment.

- **Breath as a Connector**: Shared breathing exercises can bring couples closer by synchronizing their energies and fostering a profound sense of togetherness.

- **Breath as an Emotional Regulator**: Deep breathing can help manage emotions, reduce stress, and elevate mood – all essential for maintaining a healthy relationship.

- **Breath as a Form of Communication**: Non-verbal cues often speak louder than words. When couples engage in tantric breathing, they're communicating their commitment to the relationship and each other.

Exercises to Foster Connection on a New Level

- **Synchronized Breathing**:

  - Sit back-to-back, feeling each other's spine. Close your eyes.

  - One partner initiates a deep breath, and the other follows. Slowly exhale together.

  - Continue for 5 minutes, focusing on harmonizing your breaths.

- **Face-to-Face Breathing**:

  - Sit cross-legged, facing each other. Hold each other's hands.

- One partner inhales deeply while the other exhales. Then switch.

- Try to maintain eye contact. The experience can be profoundly intimate.

- **Heart-to-Heart Breathing**:

  - Sit facing each other and embrace.

  - Try to position your hearts to be close to each other.

  - Breathe deeply, feeling the rhythm of each other's heartbeat and breath.

- **Silent Communication**:

  - Without speaking, face each other, and breathe deeply.

  - Try to convey emotions, love, and appreciation through your breath and eye contact.

Today's takeaway: as you navigate the waters of your relationship, always remember the power of being present. Whether you're sharing a meal or taking a deep breath, the key lies in sharing the moment fully, deeply, and mindfully.

Day 12: Partner Yoga Session

> *"In learning you will teach, and in teaching you will learn."*
> – Phil Collins

Imagine the physical and emotional grace of yoga. Now, amplify that image with the intimacy and bonding power of a romantic partnership. Partner yoga, often referred to as couples yoga, is a practice that invites two individuals to intertwine, support, and guide each other through various poses. By the end of this chapter, you'll understand the magic of combining strength, flexibility, and connection in this synchronized dance of love and trust.

Why Partner Yoga?

- **Deepened Connection**: Yoga inherently is a practice of self-awareness. When done with a partner, this awareness extends to the other, creating a bridge of understanding and empathy.

- **Building Trust**: Entrusting your weight and balance to another is no minor act. It fosters reliance, understanding, and the art of 'letting go'.

- **Enhanced Communication**: Physical cues, eye contact, and breath synchronization nurture non-verbal communication, essential for a relationship's depth.

- **Physical Benefits**: Besides improving flexibility, strength, and balance, partner yoga also helps correct postures as each person acts as the other's guide.

Guided Yoga Poses for Two

- **Seated Breathing**: Begin by sitting back-to-back, legs crossed. Feel the other's breath and try to synchronize your inhales and exhales. This sets the tone for the practice ahead.

- **Forward-Backward Bend**: Remaining back-to-back, one partner bends forward from the hips into a forward bend, while the other leans back onto them in a gentle backbend. Switch roles after a few breaths.

- **Twin Trees**: Stand side by side, hips touching. Both of you should place your inside foot on the inside thigh of the same leg, forming a tree pose. Raise your inside arm and press your palms together overhead.

- **Double Downward Dog**: One partner assumes a standard downward dog. The other places their hands just in front of the first partner's hands, raises their hips, and places their feet on the first partner's lower back, coming into a downward dog on top.

- **Assisted Boat Pose**: Sit facing each other, knees bent, feet flat. Hold each other's hands and lift your feet, bringing shins parallel to the ground. Straighten legs if comfortable.

Remember, the purpose isn't to perfect the poses but to feel the connection, support, and mutual growth. Adjust based on what feels right for both of you.

After the Session

Post-session, it's crucial to cool down and reflect:

- **Child's Pose**: Individually, come into a child's pose. It's a pose of surrender, gratitude, and humility.

- **Shared Savasana**: Lie down side by side, slightly touching, and absorb the energy and vibes of the session.

- **Discussion**: Discuss the experience. What did you feel? Were there any moments of revelation or discomfort? How did mutual support impact your practice?

Today's Takeaway: Partner yoga isn't just about physical postures; it's a dance of trust, understanding, and mutual growth. Through synchronized movements and breath, we find a rhythm that speaks of connection and intimacy.

Day 13: Memory Lane: Reflecting on Shared Moments

"We do not remember days, we remember moments."
– Cesare Pavese

Relationships are a beautiful tapestry woven with threads of shared memories, experiences, and emotions. Sometimes, amidst the chaos of life, we forget to cherish these threads. Today, we'll embark on a journey down memory lane, revisiting and honoring the moments that define your union.

Revisiting Relationship Milestones

- **Firsts**: The first date, first kiss, first vacation. 'Firsts' are brimming with uncertainty and thrill. Discuss the emotions, settings, and surprises of these milestones.

- **Challenges Overcome**: Every relationship faces trials. Reflect on those moments, the lessons learned, the strengths discovered, and how they shaped your bond.

- **Shared Joys**: Celebrations, birthdays, promotions, or simply perfect days. Revel in the memories of shared laughter and happiness.

- **Dreams Realized**: Talk about the dreams you've achieved together, be it buying a house, adopting a pet, or writing a book.

Deepening Appreciation for Shared History

- **Photo Album Dive**: Physically or digitally, go through your albums. Each photo has a story, an emotion. Allow yourselves to be transported back.

- **Memory Jar**: Create a jar where you both write down favorite memories on slips of paper. Read them out to each other, adding context and feelings.

- **Recreate a Date**: Pick a significant date from your past and recreate it. It could be your first date or another meaningful event.

- **Letter Writing**: Write letters to each other about a

memory that stands out, describing what it meant to you.

The Beauty of Shared Moments

In the wise words of Dr. Seuss, "Sometimes you will never know the value of a moment until it becomes a memory." Reflecting on shared moments isn't just an exercise in nostalgia. It reinforces the foundation of your relationship. It reminds you both of the challenges overcome, the joys experienced, and the resilience of your bond.

Sometimes, it's easy to focus on what lies ahead and forget the path traversed. But this journey, with its ups and downs, detours, and milestones, deserves celebration. By reflecting on shared memories, couples can rekindle feelings of gratitude, love, and appreciation for their shared history.

Today's Takeaway: Our shared history is a treasure trove of moments, lessons, and emotions. By reflecting and cherishing these, we not only honor our past but also fortify our future.

Day 14: Sound Healing: Singing Bowl Session

"Music in the soul can be heard by the universe." - Lao Tzu

The human body is a magnificent orchestra of vibrations. Every thought, every emotion, and every cell resonates with energy. For thousands of years, ancient cultures have understood the influence of sound as a healing agent. From Gregorian chants in Europe to the droning hum of Tibetan monks, sound has been a conduit for inner harmony and balance. Today, we explore the mesmerizing world of singing bowls.

The Science and Art of Sound Healing

Sound healing, sometimes termed as vibrational medicine, channels energies to rejuvenate the body, mind, and spirit. The essence of this practice lies in the vibrations and subtle frequencies it uses.

- **Resonance**: This refers to the phenomenon where one object (in this case, our body) vibrates at the same natural frequency of a second object. Essentially, through the power of resonance, sound can be used to restore the body's balance.

- **Entrainment**: Our brains have a unique ability to synchronize with sounds. With rhythmic frequencies like those produced by singing bowls, our brain waves can align, leading to deep meditation and calm.

Experiencing the Singing Bowl

Tibetan Singing Bowls, often made from a mix of metals, produce sounds that invoke a deep state of relaxation. When played, they offer a rich tapestry of harmonic overtones that enhance healing.

1. Setting the Atmosphere:

- Find a quiet space where you both can sit comfortably.

- Dim the lights and, if you'd like, light some incense or candles.

- Position the bowl between you. If you have more than one bowl, even better!

2. Techniques to Play the Bowl:

- **Striking**: Using a mallet, gently strike the side of the bowl.

- **Singing**: By pressing the mallet against the side of the bowl and circling the rim, the bowl will 'sing'.

Guided Singing Bowl Session for Couples:

- Start by taking deep breaths. Focus on the natural rhythm of your breath and heartbeats.

- One partner strikes the bowl, letting its resonance fill the space.

- Both partners close their eyes, focusing on the vibrations. Imagine it permeating every cell in your body.

- The other partner can now make the bowl 'sing'. As the sound sustains, visualize it wrapping around both of you, connecting you in a cocoon of energy.

- Continue this for about 20 minutes, taking turns playing the bowl.

Feel the waves of sound engulfing you, notice its effect on your thoughts, breathing, and state of mind.

Today's Takeaway: Embracing sound as a medium, we can touch the profound silences of our inner selves. This resonance isn't just about hearing but feeling and connecting on a vibrational level.

DAY 15: HALFWAY REFLECTIONS AND ADJUSTMENTS

"The journey of a thousand miles begins with one step." - Lao Tzu

You've arrived at the halfway mark of this transformative retreat. The journey so far, no doubt, has been enlightening. It's a mosaic of emotions, revelations, and shared moments. Today is about introspection, adjusting, and recalibrating as you prepare for the next leg of your shared journey.

Reflecting on The Journey

Set aside an hour or two, grab a journal, and sit comfortably with your partner.

- **Moments of Joy**: Jot down the days or activities that brought immense joy and connection.

- **Challenges Faced**: Not all days are smooth. Identify moments when you felt challenged or disconnected.

- **Revelations**: Have there been moments of clarity? Maybe about each other or about your relationship?

Discussing and Sharing

Communication is the backbone of understanding.

- Share your moments of joy. Relive those memories, understand what made them special.

- Discuss the challenges. This isn't about blame but understanding. Listen to your partner's perspective and feelings.

- Celebrate the revelations. Acknowledge the growth and understanding you've both garnered.

Adjusting Intentions

Your initial intentions set the stage for this retreat. But growth means change. Reflect on those initial intentions:

- Are they still relevant?

- Do they need tweaking?

- Are there new intentions you both want to set for the upcoming days?

Planning for the Days Ahead

While the retreat is structured, it's essential to remain flexible.

- **Activities You'd Like to Revisit**: Some activities might have resonated deeply. Would you like to incorporate them again in the upcoming days?

- **Activities to Modify**: Perhaps some activities could be adjusted to better suit your needs.

- **New Ideas**: Maybe there's something new you both want to try!

Today's Takeaway: The journey is as much about introspection as it is about moving forward. By understanding our past steps, we're better equipped to step into tomorrow. Here's to the next chapter of your shared adventure!

Day 16: Art Therapy: Painting Emotions

Stepping into Day 16, we're going to embrace an artistic approach to understanding, expressing, and connecting. At the heart of a deep, meaningful relationship is the willingness to be vulnerable and to share our most authentic selves, our raw emotions, our dreams, and our fears. Today, we'll use art as a medium to convey what words sometimes can't capture.

Why Painting?

Art has long been used as a form of therapy. For many, it provides a safe space to communicate feelings and experiences that may be too challenging or complicated to articulate verbally. When we paint:

- We bypass the analytical mind and speak directly from the heart.

- It allows for self-exploration and self-expression.

- Painting together creates a shared, non-verbal dialogue.

Crafting Your Artistic Space

Before we dive into the painting activity, it's essential to set the scene:

- Find a quiet, comfortable space.

- Lay down newspapers or a drop cloth to prevent any paint spills.

- Use paints (watercolor, acrylics, or any medium you prefer), brushes, and canvases or paper.

- Create a shared palette of colors and ensure both of you have easy access.

- Play some calming background music if you wish.

Activity: Painting Your Emotions

- **Step 1:** Begin with deep breaths. Ground yourselves in

the present moment.

- **Step 2:** Think of a significant moment or emotion in your relationship – it could be joy, fear, love, hope, or any other feeling.

- **Step 3:** Without discussing what you've chosen, start painting. Let the colors and strokes represent your emotion.

- **Step 4:** Once finished, take turns to interpret each other's artwork. This moment offers a chance to understand your partner's perspective without preconceived notions.

Sharing and Discussing Created Artworks

After interpreting each other's artworks, discuss:

- The emotion or memory you tried to convey.

- The colors chosen and their significance.

- The process – did it evoke new emotions or insights?

Today's takeaway: Art serves as a mirror to our soul, reflecting our deepest emotions and desires. Sharing this with our partner strengthens our bond and deepens our understanding of one another.

Day 17: Holistic Movie Night

Day 17 brings a more relaxed activity, yet one that still promotes connection and deeper understanding. Film has the power to inspire, provoke thought, and elicit powerful emotions. Tonight, you'll share a holistic movie night, engaging in a relationship-enhancing film and following it up with a thoughtful discussion.

Why a Relationship-Enhancing Film?

Movies can:

- Act as conversation starters, helping tackle difficult topics.

- Provide relatable scenarios or characters that resonate with personal experiences.

- Offer fresh perspectives on love, relationships, and human connection.

Choosing the Right Film

- Select a film that both of you haven't seen. This ensures shared novelty.

- Opt for films that focus on relationships, growth, or self-discovery. Genres like romantic drama, coming-of-age, or even documentaries about real-life couples can be impactful.

- Avoid movies that might be triggering or evoke negative memories.

Setting Up Your Movie Space

- Create a cozy environment: dim lights, soft blankets, and comfy cushions.

- Prepare some healthy snacks and beverages.

- Ensure you're free from distractions, so keep phones on silent mode.

Post-Viewing Discussion

Once the film ends, it's crucial to engage in a conversation about it. Here are some guiding questions:

- How did the film resonate with you personally?

- Were there characters or situations that reminded you of your relationship journey?

- What were the key takeaways about relationships from the movie?

- Are there any lessons you'd like to apply to your relationship?

Remember, there's no right or wrong interpretation. The discussion's essence is to share, understand, and connect.

Today's takeaway: Films can be more than mere entertainment. They act as mirrors reflecting society, relationships, and personal growth. By engaging with them mindfully, couples can gain profound insights into their bond.

DAY 18: EXPLORING LOVE LANGUAGES

> "We must be willing to learn our spouse's primary love language if we are to be effective communicators of love." - Dr. Gary Chapman

Welcome to Day 18, where we dive deep into the concept of Love Languages. This insightful framework, developed by Dr. Gary Chapman, revolutionized how many understand and communicate affection. Recognizing and speaking your partner's primary love language can radically enhance your relationship's depth and satisfaction.

Understanding the Five Love Languages

At its core, the Love Languages identify five unique ways individuals express and receive love:

- **Words of Affirmation** - Expressing affection through spoken affection, praise, or appreciation.

- **Acts of Service** - Actions, rather than words, are used to show and receive love.

- **Receiving Gifts** - Gifting is symbolic of love and affection.

- **Quality Time** - Undivided attention and time spent together is paramount.

- **Physical Touch** - Physical signs of love such as hugging, kissing, and cuddling are cherished.

Discovering Your Love Languages

It's not unusual for couples to possess different primary love languages. Recognizing these can be a game-changer.

- Take the official online quiz or peruse Dr. Chapman's book, *The 5 Love Languages*.

- Share and discuss your results with each other.

- Remember, most people appreciate all the love languages to some degree. The key is finding out which resonates most.

Crafting Acts of Love

Now that you've identified each other's primary love languages, it's time to put that knowledge into action:

- **Words of Affirmation** - Write a heartfelt letter, compliment genuinely, or express gratitude.

- **Acts of Service** - Prepare a meal, tackle a chore, or handle a responsibility your partner typically manages.

- **Receiving Gifts** - It doesn't have to be grand. A small, thoughtful gift can mean the world.

- **Quality Time** - Dedicate an evening to each other, free from distractions.

- **Physical Touch** - Prioritize cuddling, holding hands, or simply sitting close.

Commit to expressing love in your partner's primary language at least once a day for the next week, and notice the transformation in your connection.

Today's takeaway: When we truly understand our partner's primary love language and cater to it, we foster a deeper, more genuine connection.

Day 19: Guided Couples Meditation

> *"The thing about meditation is that you become more and more you."* - David Lynch

On Day 19, we embark on a journey inward, turning our focus to the powerful practice of meditation. Meditating as a couple can magnify the benefits, fostering unity, understanding, and shared serenity.

Why Meditation for Couples?

Meditation has been proven to:

- Reduce stress and anxiety.

- Increase self-awareness and emotional health.

- Promote emotional connection between partners.

When practiced together, these benefits can elevate your mutual bond, heightening empathy and synchronizing emotional wavelengths.

Setting the Scene

- Choose a quiet space free from distractions.

- Dim the lights or light a candle to create a serene environment.

- Sit comfortably, either on a cushion, chair, or directly on the floor. You can sit back to back, side by side, or facing each other, holding hands.

- Play soft background music or a guided meditation track if you prefer.

Synchronized Breathing and Visualization

Start by taking five deep, synchronized breaths:

- Inhale together deeply through the nose.

- Exhale together slowly through the mouth.

Visualization:

- Imagine a ball of golden light at the center of your chest (your heart chakra).

- With every inhale, see this light grow brighter and larger.

- As you exhale, visualize this light connecting with your partner's, intertwining and pulsating as one.

Continue this visualization for 10-15 minutes, focusing on the unity and shared energy.

Embracing Peace and Calm Together

After your meditation session:

- Sit in silence for a few moments, absorbing the shared experience.

- Discuss any thoughts, feelings, or realizations that emerged.

- Commit to integrating couple's meditation into your routine, even if it's just a few minutes a day.

Today's takeaway: Shared meditation creates a sacred space of mutual understanding, elevating not just individual consciousness but also unifying the soulful bond between partners.

Day 20: Adventure Day: Planning a Future Getaway

"Travel brings power and love back into your life." – Rumi

As we approach Day 20, let's take a moment to step out of our current surroundings and dive into the realm of dreams and shared adventures. Today is about conjuring up places you both wish to explore, cultures you'd like to immerse yourselves in, and experiences you want to gather together.

The Joy of Shared Dreaming

When couples dream together, they create a shared vision, strengthen their bond, and build anticipation for the future. It also acts as a reminder of why you chose to share your life with this specific individual.

Why Plan a Future Getaway Together?

- **Strengthening the Bond:** Planning a shared experience can remind you both of why you fell in love.

- **Creating Shared Memories:** Shared experiences become cherished memories.

- **Discovering Each Other:** Traveling reveals new facets of your partner, leading to deeper understanding and intimacy.

Steps to Crafting a Future Travel Itinerary

- **Dream Together:** Begin by sharing each of your top three dream destinations. Discuss the reasons, experiences you anticipate, and what makes it special for both of you.

- **Budget Planning:** Realistically consider what you can afford. This doesn't mean you can't dream big; it's about making the dream attainable.

- **Incorporate Both Interests:** If one of you loves the beach and the other is an avid mountaineer, consider destinations that cater to both. Places like Hawaii or New Zealand offer both beaches and hiking.

- **Research:** Dive into travel blogs, guidebooks, and documentaries. Let yourselves get excited by the local culture, food, and activities.

- **Itinerary Planning:** List out places you want to visit, activities you'd love to partake in, and experiences you both find intriguing. Remember, it's about quality, not quantity.

- **Share Responsibilities:** Divide tasks based on your individual strengths. One can look into accommodation while the other researches local cuisines or cultural events.

The Emotional Journey

Beyond the physical journey, it's essential to understand the emotional layers a trip can add to your relationship:

- Discuss your past travel experiences, both good and bad.

- Talk about your travel pet peeves.

- Discuss expectations from this trip – relaxation, adventure, cultural immersion, etc.

Today's takeaway: Dreaming and planning together infuse your relationship with excitement and anticipation, setting the foundation for countless shared memories.

Day 21: Shared Reading Session

"*Reading gives us someplace to go when we have to stay where we are.*" – *Mason Cooley*

Welcome to Day 21, where we embrace the transformative power of literature. A shared reading session can be a deeply intimate and enriching experience, offering both a bridge to new worlds and insights into your partner's mind.

The Power of Shared Reading

When we read, we often resonate with specific phrases, stories, or concepts that align with our personal experiences and beliefs. Sharing these can provide a window into each other's souls.

Selecting a Chapter from a Couples-Focused Book

Choose a book that focuses on relationships, love, or personal growth. Some classics include:

- *The Five Love Languages* by Gary Chapman

- *Men Are from Mars, Women Are from Venus* by John Gray

- *Hold Me Tight* by Dr. Sue Johnson

- *The Seven Principles for Making Marriage Work* by John Gottman

Guided Steps for a Shared Reading Session

- **Setting the Ambiance:** Create a cozy reading nook with comfortable seating, soft lighting, and maybe even some light background music.

- **Taking Turns:** Decide who will read first. Take turns reading out paragraphs or pages.

- **Pause and Reflect:** After reading a section that resonates, pause. Discuss your thoughts, feelings, and what you believe the author is conveying.

- **Deep Dive:** What did the segment bring up for you emotionally? Share past experiences or beliefs that align with the reading.

- **Empathy:** When your partner shares, listen actively. This isn't about solving or debating but understanding and empathizing.

Benefits of a Shared Reading Session

- **Enhanced Understanding:** Literature can articulate feelings and situations that we sometimes find hard to express.

- **Vulnerability:** Sharing personal resonances and reflections opens up deeper layers of vulnerability.

- **Shared Learning:** Both of you grow and learn together, leading to collective evolution.

Tips

- Choose a chapter that isn't too long, so it's manageable in one sitting.

- Keep an open mind. Even if you disagree with the author or each other, use this as an opportunity for discussion, not debate.

- Consider making this a regular activity, broadening to other genres or even poetry.

Today's takeaway: Shared reading not only enhances your intellectual connection but also provides an avenue for deeper emotional understanding and intimacy.

DAY 22: ENERGY HEALING AND REIKI

"Energy and persistence conquer all things." – Benjamin Franklin

Introducing the Basics of Reiki

Reiki is a Japanese term that can be broken down into two parts: "Rei" means "higher power" or "spiritual power," and "Ki" means "life force energy." When combined, Reiki translates to "spiritually guided life force energy." This energy healing practice involves the transfer of universal energy from the practitioner's palms to their patient, promoting emotional or physical healing.

While it may sound mystical, Reiki has gained popularity in the West over the past few decades, with many attesting to its tangible benefits. Like a couple's massage but with energy instead of touch, couples Reiki can be a deeply intimate and connecting experience.

- **History**: Mikao Usui, a Japanese Buddhist, developed Reiki in the early 20th century. While it's a relatively modern practice, it draws upon ancient ideas about energy and healing.

- **Principles**: The core of Reiki revolves around five principles:

  - Just for today, I will not be angry.

  - Just for today, I will not worry.

  - Just for today, I will be grateful.

  - Just for today, I will do my work honestly.

  - Just for today, I will be kind to every living thing.

Sharing Energy and Healing with Each Other

For couples, Reiki can be an opportunity to deepen their connection through the act of giving and receiving energy. This practice encourages vulnerability, trust, and openness. Here's a beginner's guide to experiencing Reiki as a couple:

- **Creating a Safe Space**: Choose a quiet, dimly lit room. You can light candles, play soft instrumental music, or use essential oils to set the ambiance.

- **Starting with Intention**: Sit facing each other, legs crossed, and take a few deep breaths. Set an intention for this session, whether it's to deepen your connection, heal past hurts, or simply relax and rejuvenate.

- **Hand Positions**: While there are many specific hand positions in Reiki, beginners can start by simply placing their hands on areas where their partner feels tension or emotional discomfort. For example, if your partner has been experiencing headaches, you might place your hands on their temples. Trust your intuition.

- **The Exchange**: Close your eyes, and visualize warm, healing energy flowing from your palms into your partner. This energy can be imagined as light, warmth, or even a gentle current. Swap roles after 15-20 minutes.

- **Closing the Session**: Once both of you have had a turn, sit facing each other again. Hold hands and take a few deep breaths, allowing the shared energy to circulate between you. Thank your partner for the energy exchange.

Today's takeaway: Reiki is more than just an energy exchange; it's a practice of trust, vulnerability, and deep connection. By channeling healing energy to one another, couples can forge a bond that transcends the physical.

Day 23: Daily Connection Rituals

"We are what we repeatedly do. Excellence, then, is not an act, but a habit." - Aristotle

Cultivating Habits for Daily Bonding

In the rush of daily life, it's easy for couples to drift apart, not due to a lack of love, but simply because of a lack of intentional connection. Daily rituals, no matter how small, can act as anchors, keeping your relationship grounded and intimate amidst the chaos.

Here are some rituals that can help:

- **Morning Check-ins**: Before the day starts, take a few moments to share your anticipated highs and lows for the day ahead. This small act can ensure you both start the day feeling seen and understood.

- **Shared Meals**: Even if it's just one meal, make it a point to eat together without the distractions of TV or phones. Use this time to talk, share, and connect.

- **Gratitude Sharing**: Every night, share one thing you're grateful for about the other person. It could be something they did that day or just a quality you appreciate.

Incorporating Small Acts of Love into Everyday Life

Acts of love don't always have to be grand gestures. Often, it's the small, consistent actions that make the most significant difference.

- **Love Notes**: Leave a note for your partner to find – in their lunchbox, on the bathroom mirror, or even tucked inside their shoe.

- **Random Acts of Kindness**: Bring your partner a cup of coffee without them asking, or take over a chore they dislike.

- **Touch**: A random hug, a pat on the back, or just holding hands can do wonders to increase oxytocin (the love hormone) levels.

- **Active Listening**: Once a day, take a few minutes to listen to your partner – really listen, without interrupting, judging, or formulating a response.

- **Shared Laughter**: Share a joke, watch a short comedy clip, or reminisce about a funny memory. Shared laughter is a potent connector.

- **Bedtime Ritual**: Before sleeping, ensure you have a consistent routine, whether it's saying "I love you," sharing a kiss, or simply discussing your favorite part of the day.

Remember, the key isn't to incorporate all these rituals but to find a few that resonate most with you and make them non-negotiable in your daily life.

Today's takeaway: Daily connection rituals are the threads that weave the fabric of a deep, enduring relationship. Small, consistent acts of love and connection can fortify a relationship against life's inevitable storms.

Day 24: Emotional Release through Writing

> *"Words can inspire. And words can destroy. Choose yours well."* - Robin Sharma

There's a raw, visceral power that emerges when we put pen to paper. Words flow, capturing the very essence of our thoughts, dreams, fears, and, most importantly, our feelings. Today, we harness this power to encourage an emotional release, forging a deeper connection with our partner.

The Power of Written Expression

Writing has long been recognized as a therapeutic tool. Whether it's a diary, letters, or even poetry, the act of putting our emotions into words can bring about profound clarity and catharsis. For couples, writing can:

- Serve as a reflection on one's feelings without external interruptions.

- Offer a safe space to express thoughts that might be difficult to verbalize.

- Act as a tangible record of personal growth and feelings over time.

Letters to Each Other

A letter can be a heartfelt mode of communication, especially in today's digital age where immediate responses are the norm. Taking the time to write to each other can foster patience, understanding, and a deep appreciation for the nuances of your relationship.

- **Set the Scene:** Find a quiet space where you both can write. Light a candle, play soft music, or whatever helps you get into a contemplative mood.

- **Write Without Judgement:** Let your emotions flow. Don't censor your thoughts. This is your personal space of expression.

- **Seal It:** Once done, place your letters in envelopes. Exchange them with your partner, but don't open them just yet!

Sharing and Discussion

After a set amount of time (perhaps an hour or so to reflect), come together in a comfortable space. Open the letters and read them silently. As you read, consider:

- The emotions you feel while reading your partner's words.

- Any immediate reflections or reactions.

- The intentions behind your own words and your partner's.

Then, openly discuss what you've written. Remember, this isn't a space for blame or argument. It's a space for understanding, compassion, and mutual growth.

Benefits of this Exercise

- **Deepened Understanding:** Sometimes, emotions are better processed when they're read rather than heard.

- **Enhanced Vulnerability:** Sharing innermost feelings requires courage and can greatly strengthen trust.

- **Clearer Communication:** Writing provides a moment of pause, allowing for more deliberate expression.

Today's takeaway: Writing can be an intimate act, capturing the essence of our feelings. When shared with a partner, it creates a space of mutual vulnerability, deepening the bond between two souls.

Day 25: Exploring Global Love Rituals

> "*Love is an endless act of forgiveness. Forgiveness is the key to action and freedom.*" - Maya Angelou

Love is universal, yet every culture has its unique way of expressing it. Today, we'll embark on a global journey, exploring how different cultures celebrate love and union. In doing so, we'll discover new rituals that can add depth and global perspectives to our relationship.

A Journey Through Worldly Love Customs

- **China - Love Locks:** On the Huxin Island of Lake Tai, couples write their names on a lock, attach it to the railing, and then throw the key into the lake, symbolizing eternal love.

- **India - Karva Chauth:** Wives fast from sunrise to moonrise, praying for their husbands' longevity.

- **South Africa - Love Bracelets:** Zulu women gift beaded bracelets to their beloved, where each color and pattern tells a different love story.

- **Wales - Love Spoons:** Hand-carved wooden spoons are given as a symbol of one's intention to feed and care for their loved one.

Trying Out a Ritual Together

- **Choose a Ritual:** From the aforementioned rituals or any others you discover, choose one that resonates with both of you.

- **Understand Its Roots:** Delve into its origin and the cultural significance behind it. It's important to approach this with respect and not appropriate, but rather appreciate.

- **Personalize:** Adapt the ritual to suit your relationship. This could mean creating your version of a love spoon, or setting your personal intentions while trying Karva Chauth.

The Beauty of Incorporating Love Rituals

- **Enhanced Connection:** Sharing a ritual, especially one from a culture different from your own, can be a beautiful bonding experience.

- **Broadened Horizons:** Understanding global love customs can lead to a deeper appreciation of the diverse ways love is celebrated.

- **A Touch of Novelty:** New experiences can reignite passion and excitement in a relationship.

Further Exploration

The world is rich with traditions. Consider:

- Reading books or watching documentaries about global love customs.

- Attending cultural festivals or workshops together.

- Speaking with friends or family from different backgrounds about their personal love rituals.

Today's takeaway: Love is the universal language. When we explore its different dialects, we not only enrich our understanding of the world but also add depth and texture to our own relationship.

Day 26: Home Sanctuary Creation

"The home should be the treasure chest of living." - Le Corbusier

Our surroundings have a significant impact on our mental and emotional well-being. The spaces we inhabit, especially our homes, can either uplift or drain our energies. Today, we'll embark on a journey of crafting a shared space within your home, a sanctuary, that becomes a testament to your connection and love for each other. This space will serve as a daily retreat, reminding you of the beautiful moments you've shared and the holistic journey you've undertaken.

1. The Importance of a Home Sanctuary

- *A Place of Refuge*: Amidst the hustle and bustle of daily life, your home sanctuary becomes a haven, allowing you both to reconnect, reflect, and rejuvenate.

- *A Daily Reminder*: Whenever you step into this space, you're reminded of your shared goals, dreams, and the commitment you've made to nurture your bond.

- *Promotes Mindfulness and Intimacy*: It's a spot specifically designed for shared moments, meditation, and deep conversations.

2. Choosing the Perfect Spot

- *Intimacy over Size*: It doesn't have to be a large space. A small cozy corner can often be more intimate and meaningful.

- *Natural Light*: Opt for a place with abundant natural light. Sunlight has healing properties and promotes positivity.

- *Away from Chaos*: Choose a quieter spot, away from the main traffic areas in your home.

3. Designing Your Sanctuary

- *Comfort is Key*: Incorporate soft furnishings like cushions, blankets, and rugs. These not only add comfort but warmth too.

- *Nature's Touch*: Bring in plants. They purify the air

and introduce a touch of nature, promoting tranquility.

- *Personal Artifacts*: Include pictures, mementos, or anything that holds sentimental value for both of you.

- *Subtle Lighting*: Soft lighting, perhaps from candles or fairy lights, can create a dreamy atmosphere.

4. Rituals in Your Sanctuary

- *Daily Reflections*: Dedicate a few minutes every day to sit together, hold hands, and reflect on your day.

- *Meditative Moments*: Use the space for shared meditation sessions. The energy you both create will consecrate the space.

- *Dream and Plan*: This is your sacred spot for planning your future, discussing dreams, and setting relationship goals.

Today's takeaway: Creating a shared space at home deepens the bond, offers a daily retreat, and acts as a constant reminder of your shared journey and commitment.

Day 27: Vision Board Creation

"The best way to predict your future is to create it." - Abraham Lincoln

Vision boards serve as a powerful visualization tool, helping manifest dreams into reality. Today, you'll craft a tangible representation of your shared goals and aspirations. This hands-on activity will not only bring your dreams to the forefront but also make you both accountable to each other in achieving them.

1. The Power of Visualization

- *Manifesting Dreams*: When you visualize your dreams, you send positive energies to the universe, drawing them closer to fruition.

- *Shared Accountability*: Putting your dreams on a board makes them more tangible and real, pushing you both to work towards them actively.

- *Strengthening Connection*: Discussing your shared dreams and aspirations can be a deeply bonding experience.

2. Gathering Materials

- *Canvas or Corkboard*: This will be the base of your vision board.

- *Magazines and Printouts*: Collect these for images, quotes, and inspirations.

- *Scissors, Glue, and Pins*: Basic necessities for your crafting session.

- *Markers and Stickers*: To add personal touches and highlight certain goals.

3. Crafting Your Vision Board

- *Dream Together*: Begin by discussing what you both envision for your future. It could be places you wish to visit, experiences you long for, or milestones you hope to achieve.

- *Prioritize*: Not every dream may fit on the board, and

that's okay. Prioritize what truly matters to both of you.

- *Organize and Design*: Lay out your images and quotes before gluing or pinning them. This allows you to play with the design and make it visually appealing.

- *Personal Touch*: Leave spaces for personal notes or drawings. It adds a unique touch to your board.

4. Placing and Updating Your Vision Board

- *Visible Spot*: Your vision board should be placed in an area where you'll see it daily. Perhaps in your bedroom or your newly created sanctuary.

- *Regular Reflection*: Spend time occasionally discussing the goals on your board and celebrating the ones you've achieved.

- *Stay Open to Evolution*: As time passes, your aspirations might change. It's okay to update, add, or remove things from your vision board to reflect your current dreams.

Today's takeaway: A vision board serves as a daily reminder of your shared dreams and pushes you both to work collaboratively towards turning them into reality.

Day 28: Embracing Silence: Silent Day

"Silence isn't empty, it's full of answers." - Unknown

As we've journeyed through this retreat, you've learned numerous ways to connect, communicate, and grow together. Today, let's embrace a different approach – *the power of silence.* Silence, in its profound stillness, can often convey emotions, understanding, and intimacy in ways words might fall short.

The Power of Non-Verbal Communication

It's been said that over 90% of communication is non-verbal. This means that our body language, facial expressions, gestures, and even the spaces in between words can convey deep meaning.

- *Understanding Gestures:* Whether it's a hand on the

shoulder or a gentle smile, gestures can express a multitude of emotions.

- *Eyes – The Window to the Soul*: Often, a mere look can say more than a thousand words.

- *The Intimacy of Touch*: Holding hands or cuddling can foster connection and provide reassurance.

Connecting Deeply Without Words

- **Silent Breakfast**: Begin your day by preparing and having breakfast together in silence. Use this time to be fully present, noting the sensations, tastes, and the simple joys of being together.

- **Silent Walk**: Take a walk hand-in-hand without speaking. Immerse yourselves in nature, absorb the surroundings, and feel the bond strengthening without uttering a word.

- **Gazing Exercise**: Sit facing each other. Look into each other's eyes for several minutes. This might feel awkward initially, but soon, it becomes a deeply connecting experience as you journey into each other's souls.

- **Silent Activities**: Engage in activities that don't require talking, like solving a puzzle, drawing, or even dancing. Feel the rhythm of being in sync without verbal guidance.

Challenges and Reflections

Silence might bring forth suppressed emotions or thoughts. It's okay. This is a time to introspect and later discuss what arose during your silent day.

Today's Takeaway: Silence can be a profound communicator, building intimacy in ways words sometimes cannot. Embrace the unspoken bond.

Day 29: Recap and Reflection

"Life can only be understood backwards; but it must be lived forwards." - Søren Kierkegaard

The tapestry of love is woven with threads of shared experiences, challenges, joys, and learning. Today, as you stand on the cusp of completing this 30-day retreat, let's look back, appreciate the colors and patterns that have emerged, and anticipate the designs yet to unfold.

Revisiting the Month's Activities

- **Memory Lane Walk**: Designate a space in your home or outside where you create a timeline of the month, using photos, trinkets, or even just notes. Walk through it together, discussing each day.

- **Journal Reflections**: Sit side by side, sipping a warm beverage, and take turns reading aloud select entries from your journals. It's beautiful to see how emotions ebbed, flowed, and transformed over time.

- **Activity Highlight Reel**: Create a short video or slideshow of your retreat, capturing memorable moments. Watching it together can be a touching experience.

Discussing Growth, Revelations, and Cherished Moments

- **Breakthrough Bench**: Find a cozy spot, perhaps under a tree or by a window, and dub it your "Breakthrough Bench" for the day. Here, share moments that brought unexpected revelations.

- **Laughter Lounge**: Dedicate time to reminisce about the light-hearted moments, the silly mistakes, and the joyful discoveries that sparked laughter.

- **Gratitude Gazebo**: Perhaps in your backyard or living room, talk openly about the aspects of each other you've grown to appreciate more during the retreat.

The Vision for Tomorrow and Beyond

The culmination of this retreat is a celebration. Discuss together:

- **Music Playlist**: Curate a playlist that symbolizes your journey. Choose songs that remind you of specific days or feelings.

- **Celebration Menu**: Plan a special dinner. Maybe recreate dishes from the nutritional cooking day or introduce new recipes that reflect your rejuvenated bond.

Today's Takeaway: Every thread of experience, be it joy, challenge, or discovery, has added depth and richness to your tapestry of love.

Day 30: Celebration of Renewed Connection

"In every end, there is also a beginning." - Libba Bray

Today isn't just the conclusion of your retreat but a jubilant beginning of a renewed journey together. Celebrate not just the milestones achieved but also the promise of countless ones ahead.

Acknowledging Efforts and Growth

- **Wall of Affirmations**: Create a wall or board where you both pin up affirmations or appreciative notes for each other. This visual testament can stay up as a reminder of your journey.

- **Reflection Ritual**: Sit facing each other. Reflect on a significant moment from each day of the retreat, expressing gratitude and admiration for the way both of you embraced the experience.

- **Gift Exchange**: Think of thoughtful gifts for each other. Perhaps a journal for continued reflections or an item that holds symbolic meaning from the retreat.

Embracing the Next Phase

- **Growth Garden**: Plant a tree or a flower, symbolizing the growth in your relationship. Tend to it, letting it remind you of your journey and the importance of nurturing love.

- **Future Retreat Calendar**: Chart out future dates, whether for weekend retreats or evening pauses, ensuring you continue the practice of intentional connection.

- **Commitment Cards**: Write down pledges to each other, promising continued effort, understanding, and growth. Store these in a special place, revisiting them annually or during challenging times.

The Grand Celebration

Tonight is special. Transform your living space into a haven of love:

- **Memory Lane Corridor**: Using fairy lights, photos, and trinkets from the past month, create a walkway that takes you both down memory lane.

- **Dance of Love**: With your curated playlist, dance under the stars or in your living room, feeling the rhythm of your rejuvenated connection.

- **Toast of Promise**: Conclude with a toast. Celebrate the past, the present, and the exhilarating journey that awaits.

Today's Takeaway: This retreat was a chapter. Your story, filled with love, understanding, and shared dreams, is an ever-unfolding masterpiece. Embrace each moment, and let your shared narrative shine brilliantly.

Conclusion: Embracing the Journey Ahead

"There is no end to the adventures we can have if only we seek them with our eyes open." - Jawaharlal Nehru

As the sun sets on this 30-day retreat, you may be flooded with an array of emotions - joy, gratitude, hope, anticipation. The journey you embarked upon, hand in hand, was not just about reconnecting over a month but about laying a foundation for a lifetime. The real magic lies in carrying forward the lessons, rituals, and most importantly, the intention to continually nurture and grow your bond.

**The Importance of Continued Commitment

It's often said that love isn't just a feeling; it's an action, a commitment. The last 30 days were a testament to that belief. But what now?

- **The Beauty of Everyday Moments**: The retreat may have ended, but the opportunities to connect, communicate, and grow have not. Realize the potential in everyday moments—whether it's a morning coffee, a shared laughter over a joke, or a nightly ritual of gratitude.

- **Staying Intentional**: It's easy to revert to old patterns. Stay committed by reminding yourself of the 'why' behind this retreat—the love you share, the dreams you weave together, and the challenges you overcome as a team.

- **Growth is Continuous**: Just like a tree that constantly seeks sunlight, branching out in different directions, your relationship too will seek and find new paths. Embrace them. Learn from them.

Further Resources and Techniques for Sustained Connection

- **Books & Literature**: Delve into the world of relationship literature. There's a treasure trove of wisdom awaiting.

- *"The 5 Love Languages"* by Gary Chapman

- *"Hold Me Tight"* by Dr. Sue Johnson

- *"Mating in Captivity"* by Esther Perel

- **Workshops & Classes**: Sign up for couples workshops, be it for communication, dance, or even cooking. These spaces offer opportunities to learn, laugh, and love together.

- **Couple's Therapy**: There's no shame in seeking guidance. A therapist can offer tools, insights, and a safe space to navigate challenges.

- **Retreats & Getaways**: This might've been your first 30-day retreat, but it doesn't have to be the last. Periodic retreats can be a way to reset, refocus, and reignite your bond.

Creating A Relationship Vision

Post this retreat, take some time together to envision what the next chapter looks like. It's a living, breathing vision that can evolve, but it serves as a compass.

- **Short-Term Goals**: These could range from establishing daily rituals, planning monthly date nights, or even setting communication goals.

- **Long-Term Aspirations**: Maybe it's buying a home, traveling to a dream destination, or starting a project together. Let these shared dreams fuel your daily actions.

In Times of Challenge

Every relationship faces storms. But it's not the storm that defines you; it's how you navigate through it.

- **Remember the Retreat**: In challenging moments, look back on these 30 days. Let the lessons be your guiding light.

- **Communication is Key**: Instead of making assumptions or shutting down, communicate. Often, misunderstandings are simply a lack of clarity.

- **Seek Support**: Lean on friends, family, or professionals. Surround yourself with a tribe that champions love and understanding.

Gratitude: The Heartbeat of Connection

Conclude every day with a moment of gratitude for each other. It's the simplest yet most profound act. In moments of doubt or challenge, this gratitude can be a beacon.

www.ingramcontent.com/pod-product-compliance
Lightning Source LLC
Chambersburg PA
CBHW012306240726
48656CB00008B/2574